THE GREAT CHOCOLATE CAPER

GRADES 5–8

A MYSTERY THAT TEACHES LOGIC SKILLS

THE GRADES 5–8 GREAT CHOCOLATE CAPER

A MYSTERY THAT TEACHES LOGIC SKILLS

Written by Mary Ann Carr

Prufrock Press Inc.
Waco, Texas

Copyright ©2011 Prufrock Press Inc.

Edited by Sarah Morrison

Production Design by Raquel Trevino

ISBN-13: 978-1-59363-499-5

At the time of this book's publication, all facts and figures cited are the most current available; all telephone numbers, addresses, and website URLs are accurate and active; all publications, organizations, websites, and other resources exist as described in this book; and all have been verified. The author and Prufrock Press make no warranty or guarantee concerning the information and materials given out by organizations or content found at websites, and we are not responsible for any changes that occur after this book's publication. If you find an error or believe that a resource listed here is not as described, please contact Prufrock Press.

Prufrock Press Inc.
P.O. Box 8813
Waco, TX 76714-8813
Phone: (800) 998-2208
Fax: (800) 240-0333
http://www.prufrock.com

CONTENTS

PRACTICE PUZZLES

APPENDIX

ABOUT THE AUTHOR

INTRODUCTION

THE MYSTERY

Reginald Van Feisty, owner of the world-famous chocolate factory Dutch Delight Chocolates, is excited over his brand-new recipe for chocolate. But before he can manufacture even the first chocolate bar, the recipe is stolen. After questioning possible suspects, student detectives find that six of the nine original suspects have sufficient motives to commit the crime. But which one is guilty?

The Great Chocolate Caper is a mystery created for children to solve. The students develop deductive thinking skills as they learn to solve a variety of logic problems. Each problem provides an important clue in the mystery. Using these clues, the student detectives eliminate the suspects, one by one, until only the culprit remains and the mystery is solved.

THE LOGIC SKILLS

In solving the mystery, the students will:
➤ develop skills in making valid assumptions,
➤ differentiate between valid and invalid assumptions,
➤ differentiate between valid conclusions and dangerous generalizations,
➤ use syllogisms to reach valid conclusions,
➤ recognize false premises,
➤ solve matrix logic puzzles,
➤ decode a secret message, and
➤ solve table or position logic problems.

HOW TO USE THIS BOOK

The book is divided into nine lessons. Each lesson introduces one of the skills listed above. In addition, the lessons include discussions of the mystery, the suspects, their motives, their alibis or other relevant information pertaining to their involvement with Mr. Van Feisty, and other pertinent facts regarding the case.

A lesson plan for each of the nine lessons is provided, listing the objectives and the materials needed, as well as describing in detail the process to follow. Each lesson may take several 50-minute class periods to complete. The amount of time devoted to each one depends on how quickly the students master each type of problem and how involved they become in the discussions.

The first lesson is optional. In this lesson, students create their own recipe for chocolate. Solving the mystery later on does not rely on any knowledge gained in this lesson. Rather, the lesson is designed to generate interest in the mystery. If you choose not to complete this lesson, you will begin solving the mystery with Lesson 2.

Practice matrix logic problems and table logic problems are provided beginning on page 45. None of these problems contribute clues that are necessary for solving the mystery. They may be used as supplementary practice. Answers to these problems can be found beginning on page 75.

LESSON PLANS

LESSON PLAN 1:
THE CHOCOLATE RECIPE

Objectives

➢ To create an original recipe
➢ To formulate and test a hypothesis
➢ To evaluate a product based on set criteria
➢ To create a symbol and a logo for a product

Materials

"Does Chocolate Really Grow on Trees?" (p. 18)
Chocolate bar ingredients:

◇ 1 box powdered cocoa
◇ 1 box powdered sugar
◇ 1 stick butter or margarine

Hot plate, double boiler
Wax paper, measuring spoons, and a large spoon

Procedure

1. Ask students how many of them love to eat chocolate. Tell them that Mr. Van Feisty, owner of the world-famous chocolate factory Dutch Delight Chocolates, has asked youngsters across the nation to create a new chocolate bar, one that is more delicious than any they have ever tasted before.

2. Pass out "Does Chocolate Really Grow on Trees?" and read through it together.

3. Write the basic recipe for a chocolate bar on chart paper (see p. 5) and discuss how much of each ingredient would be needed to make the delicious chocolate. Would you need more cocoa, more sugar, or equal amounts of each? Discuss the possible variations.

4. Follow the directions for the basic recipe and give each student a taste. Discuss criteria that might be used to evaluate a chocolate bar. Consider criteria like sweetness, chocolate flavor, texture, and butter flavor. Ask students to suggest other criteria. List criteria on the board.

5. Ask students if they think other variations on this recipe might better meet the criteria for a delicious chocolate bar. Have each student write down the variation they think would best meet the criteria. Explain that they have just formulated a hypothesis.

6. Now, test the hypotheses by making all of the variations and testing them according to the criteria students have chosen. Determine which variation best meets the criteria. This is the recipe that will be sent to Mr. Van Feisty. You might allow the students to create their own variations, depending on the size of your class and the grade level.

Basic Recipe

1 Tbsp powdered cocoa
1 Tbsp powdered sugar
1 tsp butter or margarine

With the top half of the double boiler in place, bring water in the bottom half to a boil. Turn off the heat and put the cocoa, sugar, and butter or margarine in the top of the boiler and stir until the sugar and cocoa are dissolved and the mixture is smooth. Spread the mixture onto a sheet of wax paper and allow it to harden, about 5 minutes.

Variations

Variation 1
2 Tbsp cocoa
2 Tbsp sugar
1 tsp butter or margarine

Variation 2
2 Tbsp cocoa
1 Tbsp sugar
1 tsp butter or margarine

Variation 3
1 Tbsp cocoa
2 Tbsp sugar
1 tsp butter or margarine

Variation 4
1 Tbsp cocoa
2 Tbsp sugar
2 tsp butter or margarine

1. Discuss names of various products. Create an appropriate name for the new chocolate bar. Discuss logos of various products. Ask each student to design a logo for the new bar. Select one to be the official logo.

2. Discuss packaging of various products, particularly the colors used, the visual effects, and the marketing strategies employed. Ask each student to design a package wrapper for the new bar, using the logo in the design. Either tell students that the bar will have a variety of wrappings, so that all of the students' designs will be used, or have the class select an official wrapper from all of the student entries after determining criteria for effective candy bar wrappers.

3. Tell students that all chocolate manufacturers keep their original recipes a secret. Discuss the reasons for this secrecy. Ask students not to give the recipe to anyone. Place the recipe, the logo, and the wrapper in a large envelope for safekeeping.

LESSON PLAN 2:
EVIDENCE AT THE CRIME SCENE

Objectives

➢ To introduce the crime
➢ To determine the crime's potential implications for Dutch Delight Chocolates
➢ To investigate as detectives, asking what, when, where, how, who, and why questions about the crime
➢ To differentiate between valid and invalid assumptions

Materials

"Secret Recipe Stolen" (p. 19)
"Evidence Found at the Scene of the Crime" (p. 20)
"Two Kinds of Assumptions" (p. 21)
"More Valid Assumptions" (p. 22)
Wall chart paper

Preliminary Procedure

If you completed Lesson 1, follow this preliminary procedure:

1. Tell students Mr. Van Feisty received their recipe and was planning to begin manufacturing the chocolate next week, but something terrible happened before he could make even the first bar. Give the students a copy of the newspaper article with the headline "Secret Recipe Stolen." Read the article together. Then discuss why this crime is serious and how it might affect Dutch Delight Chocolates.

2. Tell students that because the recipe was their creation, Mr. Van Feisty has asked that they turn in their chefs' aprons for detective badges and solve the case. They must try to find out who stole the recipe. Continue with third step of the lesson plan.

If you omitted Lesson 1, follow this preliminary procedure:

1. Give each student a copy of the newspaper article "Secret Recipe Stolen." Read it and discuss why this crime is serious. Ask how this crime might affect Dutch Delight Chocolates.

2. Tell students that because they are excellent thinkers, they have been asked by Mr. Van Feisty, owner of Dutch Delight Chocolates, to solve the case and find out who stole the recipe.

Continuing Procedure

1. Ask students what questions they think detectives must answer in their investigations. They should come up with the key words what, when, where, how, why, and who.

2. Prepare materials for the investigation. Students will need paper to record all information and a folder in which to keep papers pertaining to the case.

3. Give students "Evidence Found at the Scene of the Crime" and "Two Kinds of Assumptions" worksheets. Complete both worksheets as directed.

4. Give students the "More Valid Assumptions" worksheet. Complete as directed. After completing this worksheet, record the answers to the where, when, and how questions about the crime. Copy the answers onto a wall chart. This chart should be kept in view throughout the unit for reference. Establish the date of the crime as the day before this lesson was presented.

LESSON PLAN 3:
MOTIVES

Objectives
  ➤ To compile a list of suspects based on motives.
  ➤ To make valid assumptions about a suspect's motives

Materials
"Possible Suspects List" (pp. 24–27)
Wall chart with names of possible suspects

Procedure
  1. Make a wall chart that lists possible suspects. The list can be found on the student worksheet "Possible Suspects List." Tell students that after their initial investigation, the police drew up a list of suspects, persons who might have committed the crime. They questioned the persons on the list in order to gather facts about each suspect. Tell students that as detectives, they must read the facts and determine if each suspect has a motive, a reason for committing the crime. Explain that they cannot know for certain what a suspect's motive might be. They must, therefore, make a valid assumption about the motive based on all of the facts they have learned about the suspect.
  2. Hand out the "Possible Suspects List" worksheet. Read the directions aloud. Explain that a suspect who did not have a reason to commit the crime has no sufficient motive and that his or her name will be crossed off of the suspect list. Direct students to complete the worksheet. Discuss their results.
  3. Cross off the names of the suspects without sufficient motive on the wall chart. As other suspects are eliminated throughout the mystery, cross their names off of this chart as well.

The Great CHOCOLATE CAPER

1. Oscar Hobson
2. Imelda Castleberry
3. Nelmira Simpson
4. Jewel Treasure
5. Airedale Johnson
6. Salty the Cracker
7. Elbarno Farnsworth
8. ~~Barry Newell~~
9. ~~Benny Bartholomew~~

LESSON PLAN 4:
FINGERPRINTS

Objectives

> ➤ To identify basic fingerprint patterns
> ➤ To analyze and match fingerprints

Materials

"Fingerprint Analysis" (p. 28)
"Make Your Own Prints" (p. 29)

Procedure

1. Tell students that fingerprints were found at the scene of the crime. As detectives, they will have to analyze these prints and match them with the suspects' prints. Hand out the "Fingerprint Analysis" worksheet. Tell students these prints were found at the scene of the crime. Explain that other prints, such as those of Mr. Van Feisty, Mrs. Castleberry, and Mr. Newell, were found in the office. Because none of these suspects have sufficient motives, their prints are not considered for analysis here. Discuss why their prints might have been found in the office. (Note: Fingerprints can be found even when they are several years old.) Have students complete the "Fingerprint Analysis" sheet and discuss.

2. Ask students if the prints of all of the suspects were found. Discuss why Salty the Cracker's prints might not have been found. List the possible reasons. Remind students that as detectives, they can never jump to conclusions.

3. If time permits, allow students to make their own prints as described on the "Make Your Own Prints" worksheet.

LESSON PLAN 5:
MAKING GENERALIZATIONS

Objectives

➤ To be able to identify generalizations and reasons why they may not be true
➤ To be able to distinguish between a valid conclusion and a generalization
➤ To be able to write conclusions and generalizations

Materials

"Dangerous Generalizations" (pp. 30–31)
"Enough Evidence?" (p. 32)

Procedure

1. Explain that a valid conclusion can only be reached when there are sufficient facts to back it up. Without the facts, a generalization rather than a valid conclusion is reached.

2. Hand out the "Dangerous Generalizations" worksheet. Discuss the difference between a valid conclusion and a generalization. Discuss the example given regarding Salty's fingerprints. Discuss why this generalization might not necessarily be true.

   ◇ Complete the worksheet as directed. Discuss reasons why Salty cannot be crossed off the suspect list just yet, because his prints were not found. (He could have worn gloves or wiped the prints away.)

3. Hand out the "Enough Evidence?" worksheet.

4. Ask students what they must do now in order to solve the case. They should come up with the idea of asking the suspects more questions.

LESSON PLAN 6:
THE ALIBIS

Objectives

- ➤ To identify each suspect's alibi
- ➤ To use a syllogism to determine holes in alibis
- ➤ To identify false premises

Materials

"Alibis" (p. 33)
"Are There Any Holes?" (pp. 34–35)
"False Premises" (p. 36)

Procedure

1. Review the case and all evidence found up to this point. Remind students that the fingerprints did not provide enough evidence to eliminate even one suspect from the suspect list.
   - ◇ Tell students that they must now question the suspects and find out where they were on the night of the crime and what they were doing. In other words, they must get their alibis. Hand out the "Alibis" worksheet and complete as directed.
2. Review facts about the date and time of the crime from Lesson 2. It is important that students remember the exact date and time of the crime before considering the alibis. Look back through previous worksheets and verify the date and time of the crime. The date of the crime, you'll recall, was the day before Lesson 2 was presented. Discuss why it might be important to remember this information.
3. Tell students they have the alibis, but now they need to get more information to prove that they are true. They must search for holes in the suspects' stories. Hand out the "Are There Any Holes?" worksheet.
   - ◇ Tell students that in order to find holes (the things in the alibis that do not make sense or cannot be verified), they will need to be deductive thinkers. They can use a formula to help them with deductive reasoning. This is called a syllogism. Discuss the example on the worksheet, and then complete the worksheet as directed.
4. Ask students if they can eliminate any suspects from the suspect list after gathering this information. Discuss their answers. Elbarno can be eliminated. He was attending the chocolate convention. Cross his name off of the suspect list on the wall chart, and have students cross his name off their individual lists.
5. Tell students that detectives must always be certain that all premises are true. Otherwise, they might reach a false conclusion. Complete the "False Premises" worksheet and discuss.

LESSON PLAN 7:
CORROBORATING AN ALIBI

Objectives
> ➤ To learn to use clues to complete matrix logic puzzles
> ➤ To use clues from the puzzles to eliminate suspects

Materials
"At the Diner" (p. 37)
"Second Alibi" (p. 38)
"Witnesses" (p. 39)

Procedure

1. Explain to the students that getting to the truth of what really happened when a crime is committed is like working a jigsaw puzzle. They must arrange each piece until they all fit together and the truth is revealed. Tell them they are going to learn how to work a type of puzzle that will train them to think like a detective. In this type of puzzle, they use clues that they fit together like the pieces of a puzzle in order to find the solution. Tell them that as detectives, they need to keep searching for facts that will prove a suspect's guilt or innocence. Discuss Salty the Cracker's alibi. Even though the diner was open on the night of the crime, they need to verify that Salty was there with his friends.

2. Tell students that considering the fact that the diner was open on the night of the crime, they now need to verify not only that Salty was there with his friends that evening, but also that he was there at the time of the crime. Write the time of the crime on the board (between 8:00 p.m. and 9:00 p.m.). Hand out the "At the Diner" worksheet and have students complete it. Tell students that Mr. Beanne substantiated Salty's alibi, and they can cross his name off of the suspect list. Cross his name off of the list on the wall chart as well.

3. Tell students that detectives questioned the suspects again after they uncovered holes in their alibis. By solving the "Second Alibi" matrix puzzle, they can discover where each suspect claimed to be on the night of the crime when they were questioned a second time.

4. Tell students the detectives must now question witnesses to substantiate each suspect's second alibi. Explain that by solving the "Witnesses" matrix puzzle, they can determine which alibi was substantiated. Alert them to remember the time of the crime.

◇ Discuss which suspect was cleared. Airedale Johnson was the only suspect who was seen by a witness at the time the crime was committed. Cross her name off of the suspect list.

◇ Discuss the fact that although the other suspects were seen at these specific locations, they were not seen at the time of the crime. Their alibis, therefore, cannot be substantiated.

5. Practice matrix puzzles are provided in the Appendix. Each puzzle will not only provide more practice in solving logic problems, but will also give the students more information about each suspect. None of the information provided in these puzzles, however, is pertinent to solving the case.

LESSON PLAN 8:
A SECRET MESSAGE

Objectives
➢ To decode a secret message
➢ To make inferences
➢ To follow written directions

Materials
"Facts About the Message" (p. 40)
"The Message" (p. 41)
"A Key to Decoding" (pp. 42–43)

Procedure

1. Tell students that a new development has occurred in the crime. Hand out the "Facts About the Message" information sheet. Read and discuss. Explain to students that the forensics lab is the department in the police department that is responsible for all analysis of evidence surrounding a case. In this department, fingerprints are analyzed, as well as footprints, blood samples, tire tracks, and other evidence. A field trip to the forensics lab of your local police department might be interesting at this point.

2. Hand out "The Message" and "A Key to Decoding." Have students read each sheet silently and then complete as directed. This provides a lesson in following written directions. Explain the sheet only when necessary.

3. Discuss the message with the students. Lead them to think about these questions:
   ◇ What clue does the message give us about the motive for the crime?
   ◇ What might "plan A" be?
   ◇ What part might the administrative assistant play in the crime?
   ◇ How long has the administrative assistant worked for Elbarno? How might her length of service be pertinent to the case?
   ◇ What steps do the detectives need to take in order to follow up on this important lead? (Question the suspects to find out if they have a typewriter and if they know Ms. Mason. Examine the typewriters to find out if one of them prints a distorted "e.")

LESSON PLAN 9:
WHO DONE IT?

Objective

➤ To complete a complex matrix logic problem and, with information provided in the solution, solve the crime.

Materials

"Notes From Detective Abel" (p. 44)

Procedure

1. Hand out the "Notes From Detective Abel" worksheet and have students complete it.
2. Have students review facts about the message found on "Facts About the Message" (p. 40). From the facts that the message was typed and that it had a distorted "e," they can deduce that Jewel Treasure is the culprit.
3. Discuss Jewel Treasure's possible motive. Consider the coded message. Ask what part Elbarno's administrative assistant played in the crime. Explain that when the police confronted Jewel with the evidence regarding the secret message, she confessed and gave the following reasons for committing the crime. If she gave the recipe to Elbarno's administrative assistant, Ms. Mason, then Ms. Mason could, in turn, offer it to Elbarno in exchange for a raise and a promotion. In addition, Jewel had figured that he would have to hire her to be the spokeswoman for Elbarno Chocolates for a large salary.
4. Read the epilogue to students or have them create their own epilogues that present just resolutions to the situation.
5. Celebrate with a chocolate party.

20217555

EPILOGUE

The recipe was recovered and returned to Van Feisty. Jewel Treasure was indicted for theft and industrial espionage. Her case will go to court in a month or so. The whole ordeal made Van Feisty realize that the desire for money and fame causes people (even himself) to do things that are wrong. He vowed to make amends for past mistakes. A week later, in a joint news conference, Van Feisty and Elbarno announced that they were merging their two firms and would be making the new secret chocolate bar together. They hired Oscar Hobson to be in charge of their test kitchen and gave him a salary worthy of his talents. Airedale Johnson was hired to work in the new chocolate factory. After being around chocolate all day, she lost her craving for the candy and now craves lettuce and carrots. Nelmira Simpson was sufficiently threatened by her brief brush with law enforcement—she decided to continue her protest in a more positive and less threatening manner. Now, she politely and lawfully lobbies stores to provide displays of healthy foods that will be appealing to children. Salty the Cracker decided that his past would always haunt him unless he did something to prove that he had changed his ways. He now works in a youth rehabilitation center, counseling young people to find positive directions for their talents and energies.

STUDENT PAGES FOR LESSONS

DOES CHOCOLATE REALLY GROW ON TREES?

How is chocolate like an apple? How is it like a black-eyed pea? It does not take a detective to answer these perplexing questions. It simply takes someone who knows all about chocolate. An expert on the subject would immediately tell you that chocolate is like an apple—not only because both can be eaten, but also because both grow on trees.

"Trees!" you might exclaim, disbelieving.

"Indeed," the chocolate expert would say. "Cacao tree—a tree that grows in the warm climates south of the equator in Brazil and along the Ivory Coast of Africa." She'd glance at you, and then continue. "And chocolate is like a pea, because both grow in pods."

"But how could chocolate come from a pod?" you'd ask. "It's nothing like a pea or even a bean."

"Ah, there you are wrong," she'd tell you. "Chocolate really is a bean. A white bean called a cocoa bean. And about 30 of these beans grow in each pod."

"Do you shell them like I've seen people shell peas and butter beans?" you might ask, picturing in your mind's eye a soft pod like a pea pod.

"Oh, no, you could only open these green, red, or yellow pods with a sharp knife or a tool they use in Brazil called a machete. You really do need to learn about chocolate!" the expert would say, laughing. "Listen and I'll tell you all about it.

"After the cocoa beans have been removed from the pod, they are piled on the ground and covered with banana leaves. They are kept there for several days while they ferment and turn a brownish-red. Then they are spread out and dried in the sun.

"After they have dried completely, they are sent to chocolate factories, where they are roasted. After roasting, the beans smell like chocolate, and their shells are brittle. A machine then shells the beans and cracks them into little pieces. These pieces are called nibs. The nibs are ground in another machine into a paste called chocolate liquor.

"Baking chocolate is made from this chocolate liquor when the liquor hardens. The liquor can also be separated into cocoa and cocoa butter or made into the kind of chocolate you eat.

"Dark chocolate is made from chocolate liquor mixed with cocoa butter and sugar. The lighter milk chocolate is made by adding milk to the dark chocolate. Occasionally you see white chocolate. This isn't real chocolate, because it is not made with the chocolate liquor. Instead, it is made with cocoa butter, milk, and sugar."

NAME:_____

Daily Times

April 6, 2010

SECRET RECIPE STOLEN

Mr. Reginald Van Fiesty, owner of the Dutch Delight Chocolates factory.

The recipe for a new chocolate bar was stolen last night from the Dutch Delight Chocolates factory. The recipe was a closely guarded secret and was locked in a drawer in Mr. Reginald Van Feisty's office. Van Feisty, the company's owner, reported the break-in to police last evening.

"We were keeping the recipe under lock and key until the new candy bars were stocked on every candy shop counter in the world,"

Van Feisty stated. The company was scheduled to begin production of the new candy bar next week, according to Van Feisty. "This will certainly upset that plan," he told police.

Dutch Delight Chocolates is the world's leading chocolate manufacturer and is reported to sell more varieties of chocolate than any other chocolate company. "Though we make the best candy, indeed," Van Feisty said, "this new bar was to be even better than our best. It was to be our top-of-the-line product."

Police are investigating the scene of the crime and are preparing a list of suspects.

STORIES INSIDE . . .

SPORTS
Jaguars Take Friday's Game   A2

LIVING
Decorating Your Library   A4

BUSINESS
Spending Allowance Wisely   B1

WORLD NEWS
Tiger Breaks Out of Zoo   C1

LOCAL NEWS
Cat Burglar on the Loose   D1

EVIDENCE FOUND AT THE SCENE OF THE CRIME

The first patrol officer at the scene of the crime found the following items on Mr. Van Feisty's desk. Which items do you think might be important to the case and should be included in the police report?

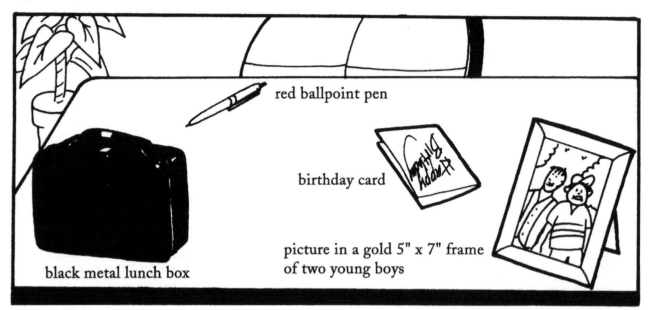

If you had difficulty deciding which items were important to the case, you probably realized you did not have enough information about each one to know whether or not it was important. With this limited information, you could only make an assumption about the items and why they were found on the desk.

An **assumption** is something that is taken for granted. It is believed to be true because of past experience or knowledge. For example, because you know that people often keep pictures of their children on their desks in their offices, you might assume that Mr. Van Feisty has children and displayed a picture of them on his desk.

What other assumptions could you make about these items and the reasons for them being found on the desk? Write your assumptions about each of the items.

1. picture: Mr. Van Feisty has children.

2. lunch box: _____

_____

3. birthday card: _____

_____

4. ballpoint pen: _____

_____

TWO KINDS OF ASSUMPTIONS

Detectives make assumptions when they are investigating a case. They are careful, however, not to rely on these assumptions as evidence until they have gathered as many facts as possible to make the assumptions valid. A **valid assumption** is one that is based on enough facts to prove that the assumption is true. A **false assumption** is one that does not have enough facts to prove that the assumption is true.

Because you did not have all of the facts regarding the items on the desk, your assumptions about them were probably false. Read the additional facts listed below, and then make a valid assumption about each item.

ADDITIONAL FACTS

➢ Mr. Van Feisty does not have any children, but his sister does. He is very fond of her two sons.

➢ The lunch box was heavy and rattled when shaken. A lock pick, a small crowbar, a screwdriver, and a flashlight were found inside the box.

➢ The birthday card stated, "To my sister on that special day. May you have many, many more Happy Birthdays!" It was signed "Reginald" in red ink. An envelope addressed in red ink to Clair Curtis in Cleveland, OH, was lying beneath the card.

➢ Several red ballpoint pens were found in the top drawer of Mr. Van Feisty's desk.

Now that you have these additional facts, write a valid assumption about each item and tell why each was found on the desk.

1. picture: _____

2. lunch box: _____

3. birthday card: _____

4. ballpoint pen: _____

Based on your valid assumptions, which of the items would be considered important evidence in the crime? Put an asterisk (*) by the items you think are important.

MORE VALID ASSUMPTIONS

Read each set of facts pertaining to the case. Then write your assumption about how the crime was committed based on these facts.

1. Mr. Van Feisty locks his door each evening when he leaves his office. "I never forget," he stated emphatically. The metal lock in the door to his office was scratched.

   Assumption: _____

2. Mr. Van Feisty locked the recipe in the bottom drawer of his desk. The drawer's lock was broken. The wood around the lock was scarred.

   Assumption: _____

3. On the night of the crime, the night security guard checked Van Feisty's office every hour on the hour. At 8:00 p.m., he entered the office, walked to the desk, and checked the locked drawer. He found nothing unusual and recorded on his report form, "8:00 p.m. check—OK." When the night security guard checked the office again at 9:00 p.m., he discovered the crime.

   Assumption: _____

4. When the night security guard checked the office at both 8:00 p.m. and 9:00 p.m., it was dark. A red light on a security panel in the security guard's room would continuously blink if the light in Mr. Van Feisty's office were turned on. The red light had not blinked at all on the night of the crime, according to the security guard. "I never took my eyes off that security panel," he stated when questioned.

   Assumption: _____

5. All four entrances to the factory were locked. A small video camera was located outside each entrance. The guard could see these entrances on the monitor located on the security panel. "I never saw anyone at any of the entrances that night," he said. The video playback proved no one had gone near any of the doors on the night of the crime.

    Assumption: _____

6. One side of the factory faced the alley. A trash can had been turned upside down and placed below one of the small windows in the factory. The glass pane in the window was broken, and the window was open. All of the other windows were locked.

    Assumption: _____

After making these valid assumptions, you can answer the following questions about the crime.

Where? _____

When? _____

How? _____

POSSIBLE SUSPECTS LIST

Read the facts about each suspect on the list. If a suspect had a reason to commit the crime, write "yes" on the line after "Motive." In the space provided, tell why the suspect might have stolen the recipe. If the suspect did not have a reason to commit the crime, write "no" on the line after "Motive." Tell why the suspect probably would not have stolen the recipe.

SUSPECTS

Imelda Castleberry

Castleberry has been Mr. Van Feisty's administrative assistant for 25 years. He has been happy with her work all those years and recently gave her a $5,000 raise.

Motive? _____

Why? _____

Elbarno Farnsworth

Farnsworth is owner of Elbarno Chocolate Company. For years his company has been losing money. It cannot compete with Dutch Delight Chocolates, the nation's favorite. Elbarno has tried one scheme after another—advertising campaigns on TV, prizes in candy packages, giveaway vacations to Hawaii and Disney World—to sell more candy than Dutch Delight. But none of the schemes have worked, and Elbarno Chocolates is still far behind in sales.

Motive? _____ Why? _____

_____

Oscar Hobson

Hobson created the original Dutch Delight Chocolate Bar 30 years ago, when he was a cook in Mr. Van Feisty's restaurant.

After selling many candy bars in his restaurant, Van Feisty decided to begin a chocolate company to make just chocolate bars. He sold his restaurant when he started the chocolate company.

Mr. Van Feisty did not give Oscar Hobson credit for the original recipe. Instead, he claimed that he had created the recipe himself. He even advertised on television that he was the person who had created the original Dutch Delight Chocolate Bar.

Van Feisty did not give Oscar a job at the new chocolate company. Oscar worked as a cook in another restaurant, all the time plotting how he might prove he was the creator of the Dutch Delight Chocolate Bar. He hired detectives and lawyers, but no one could prove his story. Eventually Oscar was heavily in debt. He could pay none of his bills, and he lost his house, his car, and finally his job. He now sells Elbarno Chocolates from a cart that he pushes around the streets of the city. He lives in a small, one-room apartment.

Motive? _____ Why? _____

_____

Barry Newell

Newell has been the night security guard for 28 years. Mr. Van Feisty recently increased his annual vacation time from 2 weeks to a month. He also gets every other Friday off because Mr. Van Feisty likes him. A picture of Mr. Van Feisty hangs on Mr. Newell's living room wall in his apartment.

Motive? _____

Why? _____

_____

Jewel Treasure

Treasure was a model hired by Van Feisty to advertise Dutch Delight Chocolates. She was frequently seen on television eating a Dutch Delight Chocolate Bar. "This is the only chocolate I would ever dream of eating," she would say in the commercial.

Six months ago, a reporter from the *National Examiner* photographed her buying a cartload of Elbarno Chocolates in the grocery store. The picture was seen on every newsstand in the country, and Mr. Van Feisty became a laughingstock. He immediately fired Jewel Treasure, saying he would see to it that she never worked as a model again. She now sells shoes at the Very Good Department Store at the Shoestring Mall.

Motive? _____ Why? _____

Airedale Johnson

Johnson is a serious chocoholic, one who is completely unable to control her craving for chocolate. She thinks of nothing but her favorite Dutch Delight Chocolate Bars and typically eats more than 20 of them a day. Although she has tried all types of treatments to help fight her cravings, all of them have failed.

A saleslady working at the Dutch Delight Chocolate shop where Ms. Johnson frequently buys her candy said that recently, Ms. Johnson had seemed desperate about her condition. The week before, Mrs. Johnson had told the saleslady that Van Feisty should be ashamed.

"He tempts people with irresistible delicacies and makes a fortune while the poor victims suffer," she reportedly stated angrily. "The government should protect us and force him out of business." Then, overcome by a craving, she had grabbed a chocolate bar from the counter, tore off the wrapper, and gulped it down. "If the government won't do it, I will," she mumbled, chewing the last bite of the candy.

Motive? _____ Why? _____

Nelmira Simpson

Simpson created a national organization that protests against the selling of chocolate to children. The organization demonstrates in front of candy stores across the nation, carrying banners stating the ill effects of chocolate.

"Children are disrespectful, unruly, and failing in school because of chocolate," Mrs. Simpson said recently on a national television talk show.

She has attempted to have Congress pass a law making it illegal to sell chocolate to minors. Congress laughed at her demands.

"I might have to take matters into my own hands," she reportedly stated to a news reporter after Congressman Dale had said she was ridiculous.

Motive? _____ Why? _____

_____

Benny Bartholomew

Bartholomew has worked his way up to higher positions at the chocolate factory over the past 15 years and is now the head factory supervisor. When questioned by police, he said he liked working for Mr. Van Feisty and stated that his boss always sent him a turkey at Thanksgiving, and another turkey at Christmas. "He also buys all my kids firecrackers each Fourth of July," he said. He plans to work at the factory until he retires at age 65.

Motive? _____ Why? _____

Salty the Cracker

Salty is a notorious thief. He was recently released from jail after serving time for stealing the design for a new video game from one company and selling it to another. As his name suggests, he is a skilled safecracker.

Motive? _____ Why? _____

_____

NAME:_____

FINGERPRINT ANALYSIS

Fingerprints are impressions or prints made of the patterns of the fingertips. Because the ridge patterns are considered individually unique, they are used by police and other authorities for identification.

Many sets of prints were found at the scene of the crime. Some matched the prints of Imelda Castleberry, Barry Newell, and Van Feisty. Five prints (marked A through E) were unidentified. Examine these prints. Study the fingerprint patterns carefully.

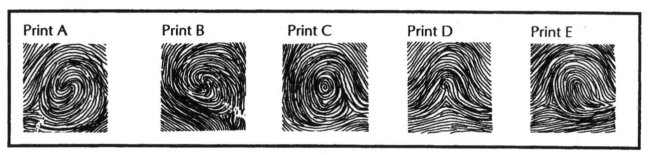

Print A   Print B   Print C   Print D   Print E

These are the suspects' prints, taken by police during questioning at police headquarters. Examine each closely. Do any of these prints match those unidentified prints found at the scene of the crime? If so, place the letter of the print by the suspect's name.

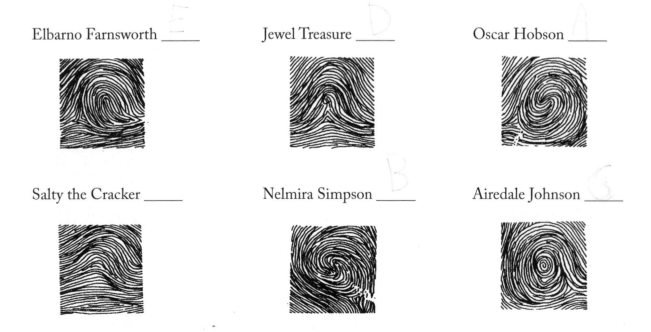

Elbarno Farnsworth _____   Jewel Treasure _____   Oscar Hobson _____

Salty the Cracker _____   Nelmira Simpson _____   Airedale Johnson _____

NAME:_____

MAKE YOUR OWN PRINTS

What types of patterns can you find in your own fingerprints? Would they be similar to or different from the patterns of your friends? Use one of the techniques described below to make a set of your fingerprints. Place them in the boxes below.

GRAPHITE TECHNIQUE

1. Using a large lead pencil, color a one-inch square on a sheet of white paper.
2. Fingerprints are taken for the part of the finger behind the nail (the section above the knuckle). Place this part of the finger on the left edge of the square and roll to the right.
3. Lift your hand and have a friend stick a small piece of clear tape on the blackened part of your finger.
4. Remove the tape and stick it on one of the boxes below. Do the fingers in order, so that the thumb's print is in the far left box and the little finger's print is in the far right box.
5. Do the same for all of your fingers.

INKPAD TECHNIQUE

1. Using an inkpad, place the part of the finger to be printed in the middle of the pad and roll to the right. For best results, get ink on three sides of your finger.
2. Roll the finger in the correct box firmly and make an imprint.
3. Do the same for all of your fingers.

DANGEROUS GENERALIZATIONS

When investigating a crime, detectives search for facts that will lead to a valid conclusion. They are careful, however, not to jump to conclusions until they have all of the necessary facts to confirm the hypothesis.

Conclusions without sufficient information may lead to generalizations. A generalization is a statement that is not specific. It frequently uses words like "all," "never," or "everybody." If there is even one exception to a generalization, it is not true. For this reason, generalizations often confuse the truth and are misleading.

These are three facts about the fingerprints found at the scene of the crime:

1. Benny Bartholomew's prints were not found in Mr. Van Feisty's office.
2. Nelmira Simpson's prints were not found in Mr. Van Feisty's office.
3. Salty the Cracker's prints were not found in Mr. Van Feisty's office.

A good detective would consider these facts. In addition, he would take into account that the police did not dust every inch of Mr. Van Feisty's office. He would, therefore, make the following conclusion:

These three suspects' prints were not found where the police dusted for prints.

If the detective did not take into account where the police dusted for prints, he might make the following dangerous generalization:

These suspects were never in Mr. Van Feisty's office.

1. Explain why this generalization might not be true. _____

_____

_____

Read each set of facts. Then write a conclusion based on the facts. Identify what is wrong with each generalization.

2. Imelda Castleberry's prints were found on Mr. Van Feisty's desk.

   Jewel Treasure's prints were found on Mr. Van Feisty's desk.

   Barry Newell's prints were found on Mr. Van Feisty's desk.

   Conclusion: _____

   Generalization: All of these suspects committed the crime.

   What is wrong with this generalization? _____

   _____

3. Elbarno Farnsworth's prints were found on the doorknob outside Mr. Van Feisty's office.

   Imelda Castleberry's prints were found on the doorknob outside Mr. Van Feisty's office.

   Nelmira Simpson's prints were found on the doorknob outside Mr. Van Feisty's office.

   Conclusion: _____

   Generalization: These suspects never stepped inside Mr. Van Feisty's office.

   What is wrong with this generalization? _____

   _____

4. From the evidence provided by the fingerprints, can you eliminate a suspect from the suspect list?

   Why or why not? _____

   _____

   _____

NAME: _____

ENOUGH EVIDENCE?

For each set of statements, write a conclusion and a generalization. You will gain more information about the suspects, as well as practice forming conclusions and making generalizations.

1. Elbarno Farnsworth is 60 years old with gray hair.
   Oscar Hobson is 63 years old with gray hair.
   Reginald Van Feisty is 62 years old with gray hair.

   Conclusion: _____

   Generalization: _____

2. Imelda Castleberry is 42 years old and overweight.
   Nelmira Simpson is 45 years old and overweight.
   Airedale Johnson is 47 years old and overweight.

   Conclusion: _____

   Generalization: _____

3. Benny Bartholomew has a small scar on his chin. He was in the Navy.
   Elbarno Farnsworth has a small scar on his cheek. He was in the Air Force.
   Barry Newell has a small scar on his forehead. He was in the Army.

   Conclusion: _____

   Generalization: _____

4. Oscar Hobson is tall and skinny.
   Benny Bartholomew is tall and lanky.
   Barry Newell is tall and thin.

   Conclusion: _____

   Generalization: _____

Evidence:

ALIBIS

An **alibi** is a statement made by suspects explaining where they were and what they were doing at the time of the crime. If they can prove that they were in a place other than the scene of the crime at the time it was committed, they are usually eliminated as suspects.

The following statements were made by the suspects and recorded by the detective in the suspects' exact words.

Elbarno Farnsworth: *"I was at a chocolate convention for chocolate manufacturers in Orlando, Florida."*

Oscar Hobson: *"I was selling Elbarno Chocolates from my street cart on the corner of 5th and Main."*

Jewel Treasure: *"I was selling shoes at the Very Good Department Store at the Shoestring Mall."*

Airedale Johnson: *"I was at a meeting of Chocoholics Anonymous to help stop the craving for chocolate I had that day."*

Nelmira Simpson: *"I was leading a protest at the Yummy Chocolate Shop at the Shoestring Mall."*

Salty the Cracker: *"I was at a reunion with members of my old gang at Lucky Luke's Diner."*

After suspects have given their alibis, their statements must then be substantiated or backed up. Whom might you question to substantiate each suspect's alibi? List the people you would question to confirm each suspect's alibi.

Elbarno:_____

Oscar: _____

Jewel: _____

Airedale: _____

Nelmira: _____

Salty the Cracker: _____

ARE THERE ANY HOLES?

After questioning suspects about their alibis, the detectives gathered some additional facts. The facts are written in a **syllogism**, a formula used in deductive reasoning.

Deductive reasoning means to go from the general to the specific, to reach a valid conclusion based on a premise. A **premise** is a statement. Two premises are written in a syllogism and organized in such a way that a valid conclusion can easily be drawn. The formula for deductive reasoning is *A is B, C is A; therefore, C is B*. It can also be written *all C are A, all A are B; therefore, all C are B.*

By following this formula, you can quickly find a hole in the alibis if there is one. For example:

Premise: All street vendors are required by law to stop selling their goods at 6:00 p.m.

Premise: Oscar Hobson is a street vendor.

Conclusion: Therefore, Oscar stopped selling his goods at 6:00 p.m.

This syllogism helps us to see that Oscar Hobson's alibi (that he was selling chocolates from his street cart) cannot be substantiated. We need to now know where he really was and what he was doing the night of the crime.

Read the following syllogisms and fill in the blanks to make valid conclusions.

1. All presidents of chocolate factories were interviewed at the convention on the evening of the crime.

   Elbarno Farnsworth is the president of Elbarno Chocolates.

   Therefore, _____

   Elbarno's alibi (was, was not) substantiated, because _____

2. All new employees at the Very Good Department Store were given the evening off the night of the crime as a reward for excellent service to their customers.

   Jewel Treasure is a new employee at the store.

   Therefore, _____

   Jewel's alibi (was, was not) substantiated, because _____

3. Because the leader was sick, the Chocoholics Anonymous meeting was cancelled and all members who went to the meeting the night of the crime were sent home at 7:05 p.m.

   Airedale went to the meeting of Chocoholics Anonymous that night.

   Therefore, _____

   Airedale's alibi (was, was not) substantiated, because _____

4. All chocolate protestors left the Shoestring Mall at 7:00 p.m. on the evening of the crime.

   Nelmira Simpson was a chocolate protestor.

   Therefore, _____

   Nelmira's alibi (was, was not) substantiated, because _____

5. All customers left Lucky Luke's Diner at 7:15 p.m. that evening because of a grease fire in the kitchen.

   Salty the Cracker was a customer at Lucky Luke's Diner that night.

   Therefore, _____

   Salty's alibi (was, was not) substantiated, because _____

FALSE PREMISES

A **false premise** is a premise that is not true. If a conclusion is reached based on a false premise, the conclusion will be false. A detective must always guard against false premises. The following circumstance will explain why detectives must be careful.

The cook at Lucky Luke's Diner stated that all customers left Lucky Luke's Diner on the night of the crime because of a grease fire in the kitchen. However, 2 hours after making that statement to the detectives, the cook checked his calendar and realized he had made a terrible mistake. He quickly called police headquarters and made the following statement:

"I told that detective I talked to earlier the wrong facts. The fire I told him about happened the day after that robbery, not on the same day. And I've got the report from the fire department to prove it."

Now, considering this fact, we know that Salty could have been at the restaurant. We know that the conclusion reached about Salty's alibi is false. It is false because one of the premises in the syllogism is false.

Read the syllogism regarding Salty's alibi and the other syllogisms below. For each one, decide which of the two premises is false and put an asterisk (*) by the false premise.

Alibis

1. All of the customers left Lucky Luke's Diner at 7:15 p.m.
   Salty the Cracker was a customer at Lucky Luke's Diner that night.
   Therefore, Salty left the restaurant at 7:15 p.m.

2. Oscar Hobson is a street vendor.
   All street vendors sell hot dogs.
   Therefore, Oscar Hobson sells hot dogs.

3. All members of Chocoholics Anonymous (CA) hate chocolate.
   Airedale Johnson is a member of CA.
   Therefore, Airedale hates chocolate.

AT THE DINER

After the cook at Lucky Luke's Diner called and reported his mistake about the date of the fire in the kitchen, detectives questioned some of the regular customers. Mr. Smith, Mr. Hobbs, Mr. Frank, Mrs. Jones, Mr. Beanne, and Mrs. Samuels were at the diner on the night of the crime. The customers arrived at the diner at 4:00 p.m., 4:30 p.m., 5:00 p.m., 5:30 p.m., 6:00 p.m., and 7:00 p.m. They stayed at the diner 1 hour, 1 1/2 hours, 2 hours, 2 1/2 hours, 3 hours, and 3 1/2 hours. Only Mr. Beanne remembered seeing Salty and his gang at the diner. Use the clues to find out when the customers came to the diner, how long they stayed, and whether Mr. Beanne could verify Salty's presence at the diner at the time of the crime.

Clues

1. The only customer in the diner longer than Mr. Hobbs was the gentleman who arrived at 4:00 p.m.

2. The customer who stayed the shortest amount of time at the diner arrived at 4:30 p.m.

3. Mr. Beanne stayed at the diner longer than Mrs. Jones but did not stay as long as Mrs. Samuels, who arrived after Mr. Hobbs.

4. The two women arrived within 30 minutes of each other; the woman who stayed the shorter amount of time arrived at 6:00.

5. Mr. Smith was in a hurry and stayed at the diner for the shortest amount of time.

6. Mrs. Samuels arrived before Mrs. Jones and stayed an hour longer.

SECOND ALIBI

Salty the Cracker and Elbarno Farnsworth have been cleared by their alibis. Detectives must now question the remaining four suspects again in order to find out where they were on the night of the crime. This will be each suspect's second alibi. The following two matrix logic puzzles will determine if any of the suspects have alibis that can be substantiated.

Detectives questioned Nelmira Simpson, Oscar Hobson, Jewel Treasure, and Airedale Johnson again. Read the clues to find out where the suspects claimed to be in their second alibis and how they reached their destinations.

Clues

1. The suspect who went to the Pepperoni Pizza Parlor did not ride a bus.
2. The suspect who walked went to the Read More Book Store.
3. Nelmira rode a bus.
4. Airedale drove her car but did not go to the Piece Good Sewing Shop.
5. Jewel remembered she had bought a new CD that evening.
6. One suspect took a taxicab that evening.

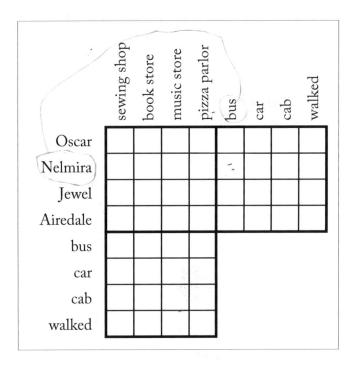

NAME:_____

WITNESSES

Four witnesses—Mr. Jay, Mrs. Pill, Mr. Toms, and Mr. Johns—each claimed to have seen a suspect on the night of the crime. Each of these witnesses were in one of these locations: the Piece Good Sewing Shop, the Rolling Rock Music Store, the Pepperoni Pizza Parlor, and the Read More Book Store. Each witness saw a suspect at one of the following times: 6:45 p.m., 7:00 p.m., 7:15 p.m., and 8:15 p.m. Use these clues to find out which witness could substantiate a second alibi made by one of the suspects.

Clues

1. Mr. Jay was not in the pizza parlor, but he saw a suspect at 7:00 p.m.
2. The witness who saw the suspect at 6:45 p.m. was in the Read More Book Store.
3. Mrs. Pill saw a suspect at the Piece Good Sewing Shop.
4. Mr. Toms saw a suspect at 8:15 p.m.

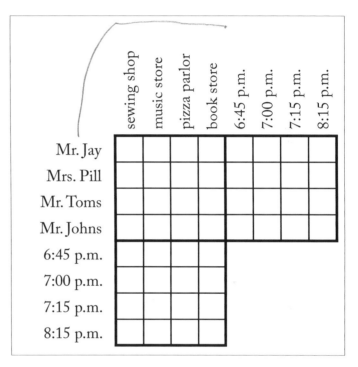

Who is this suspect, and at what time was he or she seen by the witness? After you have this information, cross the suspect off of the suspect list.

FACTS ABOUT THE MESSAGE

The police station received a phone call this morning from Elbarno Farnsworth. Mr. Farnsworth reported that he had arrived at his office at 7:15 a.m. before Delores Mason, his administrative assistant. Elbarno had written a note for Ms. Mason and was putting it on her desk. Then the mail carrier delivered the morning's mail. Mr. Farnsworth took the stack of letters and was about to lay them on the desk for Ms. Mason to sort, but he decided instead to do the job himself.

"Without realizing it, I opened an envelope not addressed to me," he said. "And I was surprised to find a coded message typed in the center of a sheet of notebook paper."

When he looked for a return address on the envelope, he discovered that it was addressed to Ms. Mason, his administrative assistant. He tried to decode the message, but after several unsuccessful attempts, he decided to call the police.

"I was afraid she might be in some kind of trouble," he stated. "She has only been working for me for a month, but she seems nice enough. I only wanted to help her if I could."

Additional Facts About the Message

The following facts were obtained after the message and the envelope were analyzed in the forensics lab.

◇ The envelope was postmarked yesterday.

◇ All letters were typed in lowercase except for the last letter of the message.

◇ The lowercase letter "e" was distorted. The top half of the loop was missing.

◇ No fingerprints were found on the letter or the envelope.

Something to Think About

1. What other information could you get from a postmark?

2. How might the distortion of the letter "e" help police?

NAME:_____

THE MESSAGE

rfc pcagnc gq kglc
rgkc rm ecr ufyr uc uylr
sqc njyl Y

Decoded message:

_____

_____

Another Message to Decode

kag mdq nqoayuzs cgufq m pqfqofuhq

Decoded message:

_____

_____

A KEY TO DECODING

If you follow these steps in breaking a code, you will find that decoding the code is easier than you might think.

1. **Write the coded message on a sheet of paper.**
   Leave enough space below each letter in the message for decoding.

2. **Search for the letter used most frequently in the code.**
   To find the letter that is used most often, list the letters you notice that are repeated frequently in the code. Count the number of times each one is used. Circle the letter that is used most often. Now circle this letter throughout the message. The letter used most frequently in the English language is the letter "e." You can assume, therefore, that each letter you circled probably stands for an "e." Using this assumption, write an "e" below each letter you circled.

3. **Search for the second letter used most often in the code.**
   Circle the letter used second most often in the message. Circle the letter throughout the message. The second most-used letter in the English language is "t." You can assume, therefore, that each letter you circled probably stands for a "t." Write a "t" below each of these letters.

4. **Look for two-letter words.**
   You know that every two-letter word has to contain one of the vowels—"a," "e," "i," "o," "u," or "y." You are lucky if a two-letter word happens to begin with a "t." The only vowel that makes a two-letter word beginning with "t" is "o." If this is the case, you can logically deduce that the letter following the second most frequently used letter is probably an "o."

5. **Make a decoding tool.**
   Most letter codes involve simply shifting the alphabet around. A common shift moves the alphabet one letter to the right. In this case, a "b" stands for an "a," and a "c" stands for a "b." Another common code shifts one letter to the left. A "b" now stands for a "c," and a "z" stands for the letter "a."

Example:

Sjmmjb eqt fetif xku zjc bpmm utujut eqt vjut
          e   e   e   e   e   e

lcuq ljgt txfpmz.
      e   e

6. **Decoding tool,** continued.

Begin by folding a piece of notebook paper in half vertically. Cut along the fold to produce two long, narrow pieces of paper. Write the alphabet vertically along the right side of one of the half-sheets of paper. Start at the bottom of the page with "a." Write one letter on each horizontal line. Use red pencil or ink to write the letters. Write the alphabet again down the left side of the other half-sheet of paper in blue ink.

To use the decoding tool, place the two pieces of paper next to each other so that the letters are aligned. You can then shift the blue letters to the right or left to align the coded letters (blue) with the decoded letters (red).

7. **Decode the message**

You know what letters probably stand for "e" and for "t" in this message. Shift your decoding tool to the right or to the left until you place the blue letter that stands for "e" below the red "e." Check to see if the blue letter you think probably stands for "t" is now below the red "t." If it is, you can now decode the message.

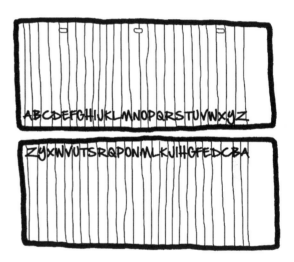

Other Important Facts to Know When Decoding

1. After "e" and "t," the most frequently used letters in the English language are: "a", "o," "n," "i," "r," and "s."

2. More than half of the words in the English language end in "e," "s," "d," or "t."

3. More than half of English words begin with "t," "a," "o," "s," or "w."

NAME:_____

NOTES FROM DETECTIVE ABEL

The coded message was typed. After questioning the three remaining suspects, detectives found that each suspect owned a different type of typewriter. The detectives examined the machines and recorded the brand name and model number of each one. The brands were No-Error, Type-O, and Type-Better. The model numbers were 124, 240, and 457. The typewriters were then tested to find out if any of them printed a distorted "e" like the one found in the coded message. Each typewriter had a defective part. One machine had a distorted lowercase "e," one had a distorted uppercase "y," and another had a broken "g." Read the clues to determine what brand and model number each suspect owned and to identify what was wrong with each typewriter. Once you know this information, you'll know who committed the crime.

Clues

1. The model number on Jewel's typewriter was 457.
2. The capital "y" on the Type-O typewriter was distorted.
3. Oscar stated that he paid only $5.00 for his No-Error typewriter at a flea market.
4. The typewriter with the model 240 typed a broken "g."
5. The Type-O typewriter was model 124.

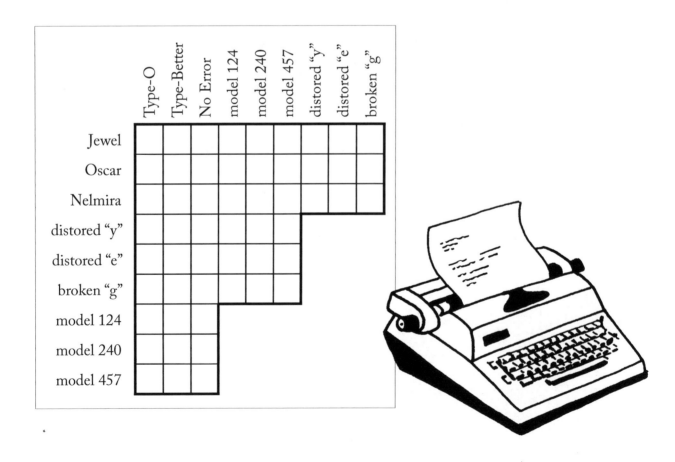

PRACTICE PUZZLES

NAME:_____

SUSPECTS QUESTIONED

After the detectives determined which suspects had a motive to steal the recipe, they questioned each of these suspects again for more information. Read the clues to determine in which order the suspects were questioned. In this problem, the words "first," "last," and "before" are very important.

Clues

1. Airedale was either the first or the last suspect questioned.
2. Jewel was the third suspect questioned.
3. Salty was neither the first nor the second suspect questioned.
4. Nelmira was questioned before Salty and after Oscar.
5. Elbarno was questioned right before Jewel and immediately after another woman suspect.

	first	second	third	fourth	fifth	sixth
Jewel						
Salty						
Nelmira						
Elbarno						
Airedale						
Oscar						

WHO QUESTIONED WHOM?

The six suspects were questioned about the crime by different detectives. Smith, Jones, Brown, Gray, White, and Woods were the detectives. Jones and White were the only women detectives. Read the clues to find out which detective questioned each suspect.

Clues

1. Elbarno knew Detective Smith but was not questioned by him or Jones.
2. After being questioned, Nelmira could not remember whether Detective Brown had brown or black hair.
3. Oscar was questioned by neither Woods, White, nor Jones.
4. All of the female suspects were questioned by male detectives.
5. Airedale was questioned by Detective Gray.

	Smith	Jones	Brown	Woods	White	Gray
Airedale						
Salty						
Jewel						
Elbarno						
Nelmira						
Oscar						

SUSPECTS' APPEARANCES

In completing a report on each suspect, the police had to record information about the suspects' hair color and eye color in addition to their names. No two suspects were found to have either the same hair color or eye color. Read the following clues and determine the hair color and eye color of each suspect.

Clues

1. Airedale has blonde hair, but not blue eyes.
2. Oscar has brown eyes.
3. The suspect with red hair has hazel eyes.
4. Nelmira has brown hair.
5. The suspect who has gray hair does not have green eyes.

	brown eyes	hazel eyes	green eyes	blue eyes	gray hair	red hair	blonde hair	brown hair
Oscar								
Nelmira								
Jewel								
Airedale								
gray hair								
red hair								
blonde hair								
brown hair								

BIRTH MONTHS

Jewel Treasure, Nelmira Simpson, Airedale Johnson, and Oscar Hobson were called down to police headquarters again for questioning. They were told to sit at a table and complete a form for police records. On the forms, the suspects were asked to give their dates of birth. The suspects were born in October, November, April, and June. No suspect was born in a month that begins with the same letter as his or her first name. Use the clues to find out where each suspect sat and in what month he or she was born.

Clues

1. The suspect born in November does not sit with a man on her right.
2. Jewel sits to the right of the man born in April.
3. The suspect born in October sits to the left of Airedale.
4. The suspect born in June sits on Oscar's left.
5. The suspect born in November sits on Oscar's right.
6. The suspect born in October sits at the 12 o'clock position.

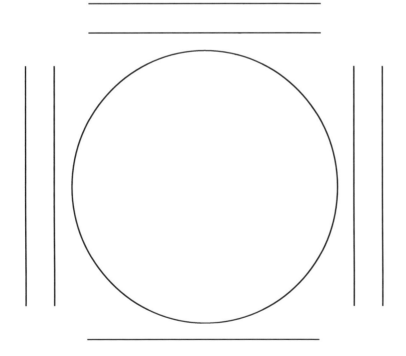

POLICE TALK

After questioning the suspects, the detective, the lieutenant, the patrol officer, and the police captain who had spoken with the suspects sat around the table in the interrogation room to discuss the case. The last names of the officers were Fields, James, Hanson, and Groan. Use the clues to match the last names with the officers' positions and find out where they were sitting around the table.

Clues

1. Groan, who sat at the 6 o'clock position, sat facing the detective.
2. The man named James sat on the lieutenant's right.
3. Hanson, the only woman, did not sit next to Fields.
4. Groan sat on the captain's right.
5. The detective sat across from the patrol officer.
6. The captain had to leave his seat to take an emergency call.

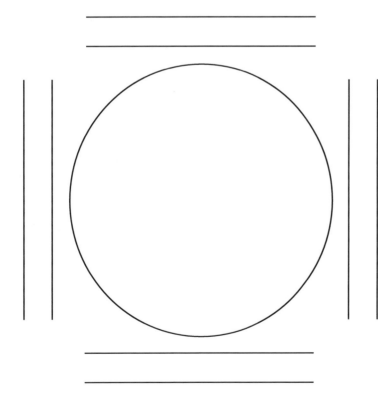

WHERE THEY'RE FROM

All five suspects—Oscar, Nelmira, Jewel, Airedale, and Salty—were born in different cities in the United States. These cities are Miami, New York, Philadelphia, Dallas, and Boston. No two suspects were born in the same city. Read the clues to find out where each suspect was born.

Clues

1. Oscar was not born in the South.
2. Nelmira was born in Boston.
3. Jewel was not born in the North.
4. Salty has never been to Philadelphia.
5. Airedale was born in Dallas.

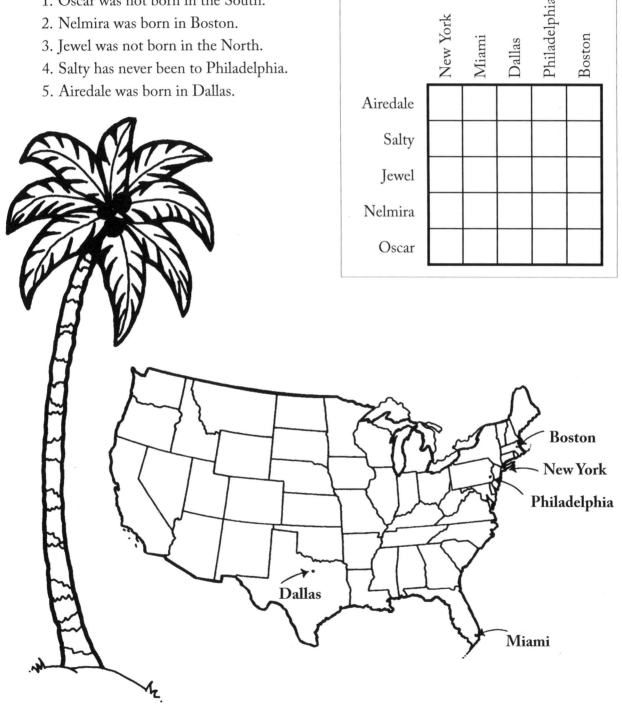

	New York	Miami	Dallas	Philadelphia	Boston
Airedale					
Salty					
Jewel					
Nelmira					
Oscar					

Boston

New York

Philadelphia

Dallas

Miami

SALTY AND HIS REUNION

Salty the Cracker and his old gang (Sly, Fingers, Shifty, and Slammer) decided to meet at Lucky Luke's Diner to talk about old times. Each gang member flew into town from a different city (Miami, Dallas, Chicago, and Boston). Read the clues below to find out where each of Salty's friends was sitting at Lucky Luke's Diner and from which city each man came.

Clues

1. Salty, who was from New York, sat on Sly's left.
2. Fingers sat next to the man from Miami.
3. The man from Dallas sat between Shifty and Sly.
4. Fingers was from Chicago.
5. The man from Boston sat next to the man from New York.
6. Slammer sat next to the man from Boston.

PIZZA BUT NO CHOCOLATE

When the Chocoholics Anonymous meeting was cancelled, Airedale Johnson and four other members of the club decided that in order to fight their cravings for chocolate, they would go to the pizza parlor for a pizza. "I can control myself with pizza," Airedale told the detectives. Airedale, Mrs. Riley, Mrs. Brock, Mrs. McGough, and Mrs. Hanes each ordered a slice of one of the following pizzas: mushroom, pepperoni, bacon, cheese, and pineapple. No two women ordered slices of the same pizza. Read the clues to find out where each woman sat and what kind of pizza she ordered.

Clues

1. Airedale, who sat closest to the door, sat across from the woman who ordered the pineapple pizza.
2. Mrs. Hanes sat between the woman who ordered cheese and the one who ordered pepperoni.
3. The woman to Mrs. McGough's left ordered a bacon pizza.
4. Mrs. Hanes is president of the club and sat to the right of Mrs. Brock.
5. Mrs. Riley whispered a secret to Airedale, who sat on Mrs. Riley's left.
6. Mrs. Brock likes cheese on her pizza, but Airedale doesn't like bacon.
7. Mrs. Brock sat between Mrs. Hanes and the woman who ordered pineapple pizza.

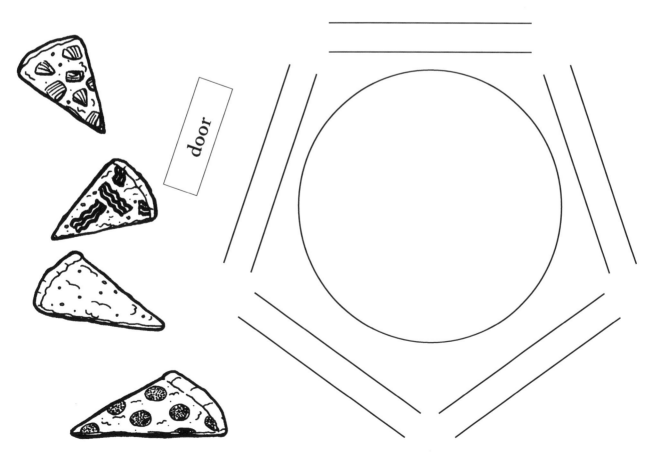

NAME: _____

POLICE REPORT — MIDDLE NAMES

The detectives filled out police reports while questioning the suspects. They asked for specific information for these reports, including the suspects' middle names. Jewel has no middle name. The middle names of the five other suspects are Hunter, Walker, Spencer, Taylor, and Bruce. From the following clues, try to figure out each suspect's middle name.

Clues

1. Airedale's middle name has only one syllable.
2. Elbarno's name is not Spencer or Hunter.
3. Salty's name is either Walker, Taylor, or Hunter.
4. Nelmira has met the suspect whose middle name is Walker, but she has never met Salty.
5. The woman whose middle name is Taylor was named after her grandfather.

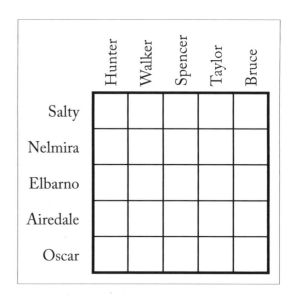

	Hunter	Walker	Spencer	Taylor	Bruce
Salty					
Nelmira					
Elbarno					
Airedale					
Oscar					

YEARS IN THE CITY

The suspects were asked on the police report how long they had lived in the city. They indicated they had been in the city for 2, 11, 15, 22, 25, and 30 years. Read the clues to figure out how long each suspect has lived in the city.

Clues

1. Oscar has been in the city longer than Airedale.
2. Jewel has been in the city less time than Nelmira, but more than Salty.
3. Elbarno moved to the city 5 years after Oscar did.
4. Airedale has been in the city longer than Nelmira.

	2 years	11 years	15 years	22 years	25 years	30 years
Airedale						
Salty						
Jewel						
Elbarno						
Nelmira						
Oscar						

TRAFFIC VIOLATIONS

The police reports indicated that four of the suspects had been charged with the following traffic violations: running a stop sign, speeding, making an illegal left turn, and running a red light. Read the clues to find out which law each suspect violated.

Clues

1. Nelmira did not run a red light or a stop sign.
2. Airedale was never stopped for speeding.
3. Elbarno made an illegal left turn.
4. Oscar was always careful to stop at stop signs.

	running stop sign	speeding	illegal left turn	running red light
Airedale				
Elbarno				
Nelmira				
Oscar				

IDENTIFYING MARKS

On the police report, the suspects listed their heights, weights, and any identifying marks. The suspects were 4'11", 5'1", 5'7", 5'9", 5'10", and 6'5". Their identifying marks were a red birthmark on the forehead, a scar on one cheek, a large mole on the neck, a crooked right index finger, a cowlick, and a widow's peak. Read the clues to figure out each suspect's height and identifying mark.

Clues

1. Nelmira is not as tall as Airedale or the woman with the cowlick but is taller than Salty.
2. Neither Elbarno nor the man with the birthmark is 5'7" or the shortest suspect.
3. Jewel is not as tall as Oscar but is taller than all of the other suspects.
4. Salty was shot in the index finger years ago and as a result has a crooked finger.
5. The woman with the widow's peak is 2" shorter than the man with the scar.
6. The woman with a mole on her neck is shorter than Airedale.

	birthmark	scar on cheek	mole on neck	crooked finger	cowlick	widow's peak	4'11"	5'1"	5'7"	5'9"	5'10"	6'5"
Jewel												
Nelmira												
Elbarno												
Airedale												
Oscar												
Salty												
4'11"						
5'1"						
5'7"						
5'9"						
5'10"						
6'5"						

WHAT THEY WERE WEARING

When the detectives questioned the suspects, they did not arrange appointments. Instead, they made surprise visits to the suspects' homes. After entering the homes, the detectives noted what each suspect was wearing. Each suspect was wearing a different type of outfit: a sweatshirt, a jacket, a vest, a plaid shirt, a sweater, and a bathrobe. These outfits were red, blue, purple, green, brown, or black. Read the clues to determine what each suspect was wearing when questioned and the color of the outfit.

Clues

1. The sweatshirt was black.
2. Neither Jewel nor the suspect wearing red was wearing a jacket.
3. The suspect dressed in green was wearing a shirt.
4. Oscar and the suspect in the brown bathrobe took a long time getting to the door.
5. Elbarno wore a sweater, while another suspect wore a purple vest that zipped down the front.
6. Nelmira jumped out of the shower and quickly grabbed her robe.
7. Airedale always wore black, and Salty wore blue.
8. Oscar does not like zippers.

	sweatshirt	jacket	bathrobe	shirt	vest	sweater	black	green	blue	purple	red	brown
Jewel												
Nelmira												
Elbarno												
Airedale												
Oscar												
Salty												
black												
green												
blue												
purple												
red												
brown												

HOBBIES AND AWARDS

When the detectives visited the suspects at their homes, they noticed their surroundings. They noted that each suspect had trophies and medals and also that each suspect had a particular hobby. The trophies and medals were for track, swimming, cooking, debate, playing the clarinet, and writing poetry. The hobbies were collecting stamps, collecting postcards, collecting baseball cards, gardening, playing the guitar, and building model ships. Use the clues to determine each suspect's prize-winning ability and hobby.

Clues

1. Neither Salty nor the man who collects stamps won a trophy for swimming, but the man who builds models did.
2. The suspect who won the Betty Crocker Bake-Off contest collects baseball cards.
3. Nelmira won a medal for playing her clarinet, but she can play only one instrument.
4. Elbarno and the suspect who won a trophy in debate do not build models.
5. Jewel enjoys either playing the guitar or gardening.
6. Airedale recently bought a rare Babe Ruth baseball card, and the man who won an award in poetry just found an old postcard of New York City.

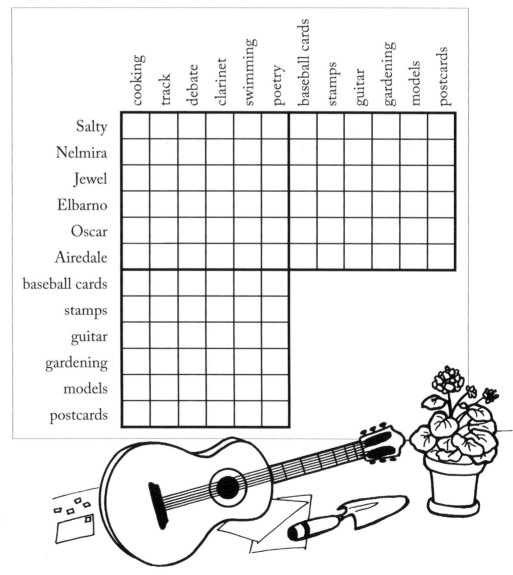

DISTANCE TO THE POLICE STATION

When all of the detectives had completed their questioning, they compared notes. One of the things they discussed was where the suspects lived and how far their residences were from the police station. The suspects lived on Bremo Road, Elm Street, Whit Boulevard, Kent Road, Stuart Avenue, and Clair Drive. Read the clues to find out on which street each suspect lived and how far away the streets were from the police station.

Clues

1. Airedale's street is not as far from the police station as Oscar's, but it is farther away than Stuart Avenue and Elm Street.

2. The only street closer to the police station than Salty's is Whit Boulevard.

3. Bremo Road is one block farther away from the station than Stuart Avenue.

4. Jewel's street is closer than Clair Drive and Kent Road, but farther away than Nelmira's street.

5. Elbarno lives on Stuart Avenue, one block farther away from the station than Elm Street and three blocks closer than Kent Road.

6. Airedale lives one block closer to the police station than Oscar but one block farther away than Jewel.

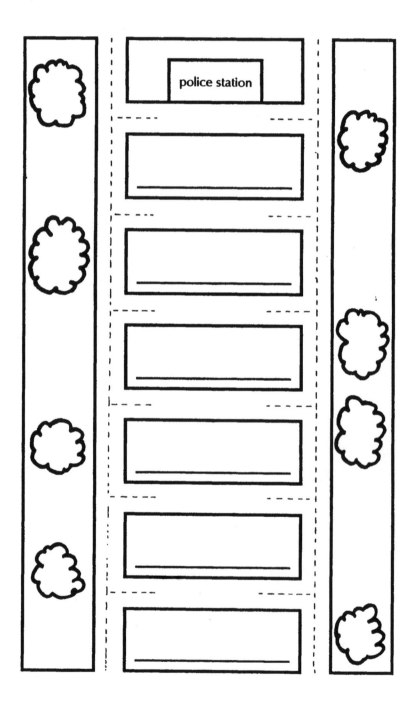

HOME SWEET HOME

The detectives not only questioned the suspects at the police station, they visited their homes. There, they noted the type of dwelling in which each suspect lived. The suspects lived in a mansion, a boardinghouse, a duplex, a cottage, an apartment, and a ranch. Read the clues to match up the type of dwelling with the suspect who lived in it.

Clues

1. Airedale lived in either a mansion or a ranch.
2. Jewel and the man in the boardinghouse lived in neighborhoods that were old and run-down, though neither of the neighborhoods was as old as the neighborhood in which Oscar lived.
3. Nelmira lived in a single-family dwelling, but her home was not a mansion.
4. Elbarno lived in either a mansion or a penthouse apartment.
5. Oscar did not live in a single-family dwelling.
6. Salty almost rented the duplex in which Jewel now lives.

	mansion	boarding house	duplex	ranch	apartment	cottage
Airedale						
Salty						
Jewel						
Elbarno						
Nelmira						
Oscar						

HOUSE EXTERIORS

When the detectives visited each suspect's home, they made note of the exterior. They noted the colors of the homes and of what type of material each one was made. The houses were white, gray, yellow, brown, beige, and red. They were made of aluminum siding, clapboard, vinyl siding, stucco, brick, and cedar. Use the clues to match up each suspect with the correct house color and material.

Clues

1. Oscar and the woman in the yellow home did not have brick dwellings.
2. Salty lived in either a house with vinyl siding or one made of bricks.
3. Airedale's house was either aluminum or vinyl siding and was either white or gray.
4. Jewel and the woman who lived in the cedar home did not have white or red houses.
5. Elbarno's mansion was gray but was not clapboard or stucco.
6. The vinyl siding was beige and the stucco was yellow.
7. The owner of the clapboard building painted it red.

	aluminum	clapboard	vinyl	stucco	brick	cedar	white	gray	yellow	brown	beige	red
Airedale												
Salty												
Jewel												
Elbarno												
Nelmira												
Oscar												
white						
gray						
yellow						
brown						
beige						
red						

SHOESTRING MALL

The Very Good Department Store, where Jewel worked, is located in the Shoestring Mall. The first floor of the mall contains the Live-Long Pet Store, the Walk-Along Shoe Store, the Read-More Book Store, the Have-Fun Toy Store, the Yummy Chocolate Shop, the Unlimited Dress Shop, the 50-Cent Store, the Picture This Frame Shop, and a food court. Use the clues to figure out where each store is located at the mall.

Clues

1. The Live-Long Pet Store is west of the 50-Cent Store.
2. The food court is on the west end, the opposite end of the mall from the Very Good Department Store.
3. The bookstore has two doors, one opening on to the south entrance.
4. The frame shop is between the department store and the dress store and across the aisle from the 50-Cent Store.
5. The Unlimited Dress Shop is across the aisle and south of the pet store, which is located by the north entrance.
6. The toy store and the shoe store are next to and east of the food court.
7. The shop selling chocolates is between the north entrance and the toy store.

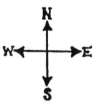

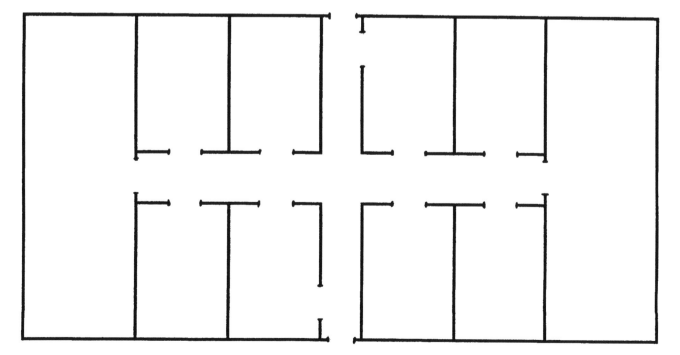

FOOD COURT

When the detectives went to the Shoestring Mall to question Jewel's employer at the Very Good Department Store, they stopped for lunch at the food court. They had their choice of food from Real Hot Chili, Triple Cheese Pizza, Please Freeze Ice Cream, Betty's Best Cookies, Horseradish Deli, General Dawson's Fried Chicken, Cornelius Corny Dogs, and Greasy French Fries. Use the clues to find each restaurant's location in the food court.

Clues

1. Jewel always eats pizza at the Triple Cheese Pizza, which is located west of Real Hot Chili.

2. Real Hot Chili is not located in a corner.

3. Greasy French Fries is between General Dawson's Fried Chicken and Betty's Best Cookies.

4. Please Freeze Ice Cream is across the entrance hall from the deli.

5. Betty's Best Cookies is between Triple Cheese Pizza and Greasy French Fries.

6. The corndogs are sold in a location that is across the aisle and directly north of the place selling chili.

7. Once you get your chili, you can go to the business to the east for an icy treat.

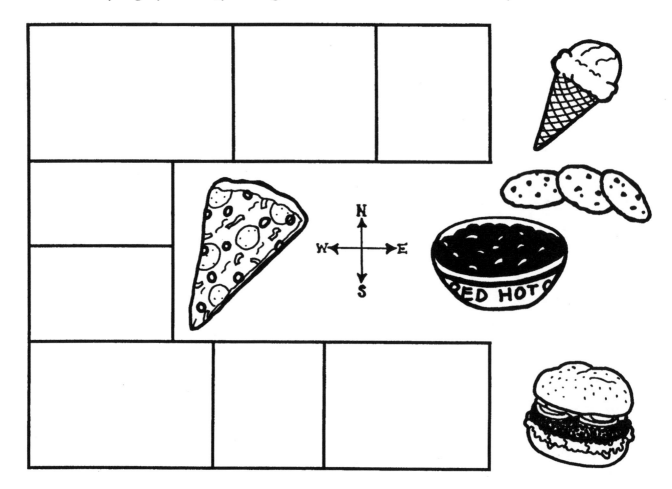

FACTORY ROW

The Dutch Delight Chocolates factory was located on Factory Row, so named because eight companies had built their factories on this road. The other companies were Elbarno Chocolates, Lint-Free Sweaters, Stay-Afloat Swim Wear, Chew-Easy Dog Biscuits, Big-Head Hats, Fit-Well Shoes, and Keep-Warm Coats. Read the clues and find out where each factory was located.

Clues

1. The two chocolate factories were not on the same side of the street.
2. Dutch Delight Chocolates was on the far west corner, across from the Chew-Easy Dog Biscuits factory.
3. Stay-Afloat Swim Wear was located between Fit-Well Shoes and Big-Head Hats.
4. Elbarno Chocolates was on the north side of the road, directly across from Fit-Well Shoes.
5. The Chew-Easy Dog Biscuits factory was next to the factory where sweaters were made.

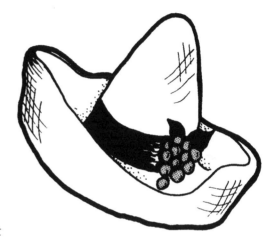

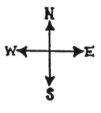

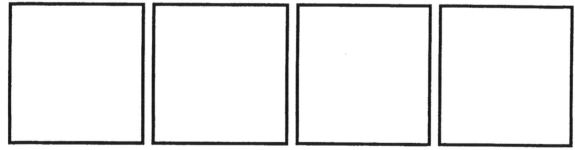

Factory Row

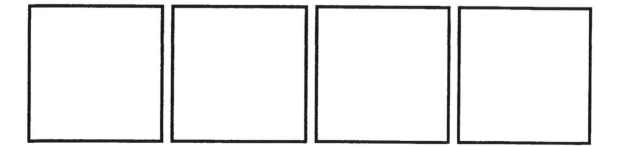

SECOND FLOOR AT THE CHOCOLATE FACTORY

Reginald Van Feisty's office is on the second floor at the Dutch Delight Chocolates factory. When police investigated the robbery, they looked for clues in each room on this floor of the factory. Read the following clues to find out where each room on the floor is located.

Clues

1. Mrs. Castleberry's office is conveniently located next to Van Feisty's office, which is located on the southeast corner of the building.

2. The supply room is not next to the conference room.

3. The testing kitchen is between the lounge and the supply room.

4. The lounge is north of the elevator, across from Mrs. Castleberry's office and not next to the lab.

5. Mr. Van Feisty frequently got the files he needed from the file room next to his office.

6. The lab is south of the supply room.

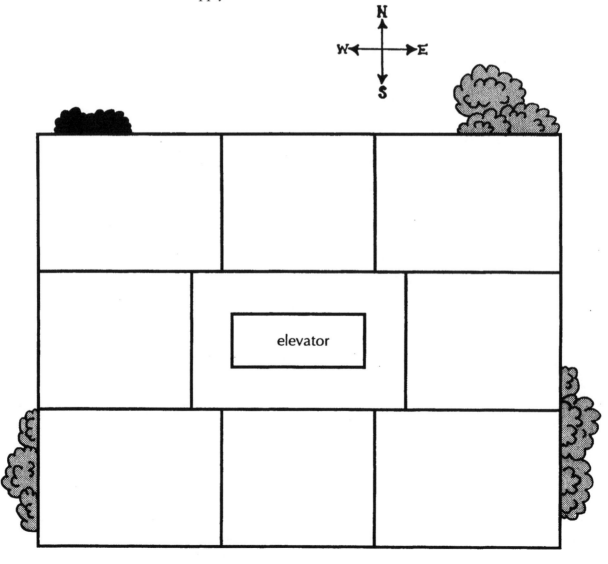

APPENDIX

THIS IS TO CERTIFY THAT

HAS SUCCESSFULLY SOLVED

THE GREAT CHOCOLATE CAPER

HAVING SOLVED THIS MYSTERY AND DEMONSTRATED
SUPERIOR SKILLS OF EVALUATION AND REASONING,

IS OFFICIALLY ACCLAIMED DETECTIVE EXTRAORDINAIRE.

TEACHER

DATE

ANSWERS

LESSONS

2.2 EVIDENCE FOUND AT THE SCENE OF THE CRIME

Likely Assumptions:

1. lunch box: Mr. Van Feisty takes his lunch to work.
2. birthday card: Mr. Van Feisty had a birthday, or he is going to send the card to a friend.
3. ballpoint pen: Mr. Van Feisty uses a red ballpoint pen in his work.

2.3 TWO KINDS OF ASSUMPTIONS

1. picture: Mr. Van Feisty has a picture of his two young nephews on his desk.
2. lunch box: The lunch box belonged to the culprit and contained items used in the crime.
3. birthday card: Mr. Van Feisty was going to send his sister a birthday card.
4. ballpoint pen: Mr. Van Feisty frequently uses red ballpoint pens.

2.4 MORE VALID ASSUMPTIONS

1. The culprit broke into Van Feisty's office by manipulating the door's lock.
2. The lock on the desk drawer was broken by the small crowbar, screwdriver, or lock pick.
3. The crime was committed between 8:00 p.m. and 9:00 p.m.
4. The lights in Van Feisty's office were not turned on by the culprit.
5. The culprit did not enter the factory through any of the four entrances.
6. The culprit entered the building by breaking through a window in the factory from the alley.
   ◇ Where?: Mr. Van Feisty's office
   ◇ When?: between 8:00 p.m. and 9:00 p.m.
   ◇ How?: by breaking through a window and using a crowbar, screwdriver, or lock pick to break the locks of the office and the drawer in Van Feisty's desk.

3.1 POSSIBLE SUSPECTS LIST

Imelda Castleberry: No; Van Feisty has been good to her and rewarded her good work.

Elbarno Farnsworth: Yes; Van Feisty is Elbarno's major competitor. He has been unsuccessful in his attempts to increase his sales.

Oscar Hobson: Yes; Van Feisty cheated Oscar years ago. Oscar lost everything in his efforts to prove he was the creator of the Dutch Delight Chocolate Bar.

Barry Newell: No; Barry is obviously fond of Van Feisty, who treats him very well.

Jewel Treasure: Yes; After being fired by Van Feisty, Jewel will never work as a model again and is selling shoes at the mall.

Airedale Johnson: Yes; She blames Van Feisty for tempting her with chocolate and threatened him.

Nelmira Simpson: Yes; Opposed to chocolate for children, she was heard saying she would have to take matters into her own hands and do something about it.

Benny Bartholomew: No; He has been treated well by Van Feisty.

Salty the Cracker: Yes; A skilled safecracker, Salty has a previous record for corporate espionage.

4.1 FINGERPRINT ANALYSIS

Elbarno: E
Oscar: A
Nelmira: B
Jewel: D
Salty: no print
Airedale: C

5.1 DANGEROUS GENERALIZATIONS

1. They could have worn gloves or wiped off the prints.

2. Conclusion: These three people had been in Van Feisty's office and had placed their hands on his desk. Generalization is wrong: The suspects touched Van Feisty's desk. However, just because they did this does not mean they committed the crime.

3. Conclusion: All three suspects had touched the doorknob on the door to Van Feisty's office. Generalization is wrong: The suspects touched the doorknob on the outside of Van Feisty's office door. This does not mean, however, that they did not enter the room.

4. No suspect can be eliminated from the suspect list. Not finding a suspect's fingerprints at the scene of the crime does not mean the suspect could not

have committed the crime. He or she might have worn gloves or wiped away prints.

5.2 ENOUGH EVIDENCE?

1. **Conclusion**: These three men are in their 60s and have gray hair.
   ◇ **Generalization**: All men in their 60s have gray hair.
2. **Conclusion**: These three women are in their 40s and are overweight.
   ◇ **Generalization**: All women in their 40s are overweight.
3. **Conclusion**: These three men have scars on their faces and were in the armed forces.
   ◇ **Generalization**: All men in the armed forces have scars on their faces.
4. **Conclusion**: These three men are tall and thin.
   ◇ **Generalization**: All tall men are thin.

6.1 ALIBIS

Elbarno: People who attended the chocolate convention in Florida

Oscar: Someone who might have bought chocolates from Oscar's cart, or someone who might have seen him selling from his cart

Jewel: Her employer or fellow employees at the department store

Airedale: Other members of Chocoholics Anonymous

Nelmira: Other protestors at the Yummy Chocolate Shop

Salty the Cracker: Members of the gang, or other diners and employees at Lucky Luke's Diner

6.2 ARE THERE ANY HOLES?

1. Therefore, Elbarno was interviewed at the convention on the evening of the crime.
   ◇ Elbarno's alibi was substantiated, because he was at the convention and could not have committed the crime.
2. Therefore, Jewel was given the evening off for a reward on the night of the crime.
   ◇ Jewel's alibi was not substantiated, because she was not at work and could have committed the crime.
3. Therefore, Airedale did not attend the Chocoholic Anonymous meeting because it was cancelled.
   ◇ Airedale's alibi was not substantiated, because she did not attend the meeting and could have committed the crime.

4. Therefore, Nelmira left the Shoestring Mall at 7:00 p.m. on the night of the crime.

   ◇ Nelmira's alibi was not substantiated, because she left the mall before the crime was committed. Therefore, she could have committed the crime.

5. Salty left Lucky Luke's Diner at 7:15 p.m. on the night of the crime.

   ◇ Salty's alibi was not substantiated, because he was not at the diner when the crime was committed. Therefore, he could have committed the crime.

6.3 FALSE PREMISES

1. All customers left Lucky Luke's Diner at 7:15 p.m. that evening.
2. All street vendors sell hot dogs.
3. All members of Chocoholics Anonymous hate chocolate.

7.1 AT THE DINER

Mr. Smith: 4:30 p.m., 1 hour
Mr. Frank: 4:00 p.m., 3 1/2 hours
Mr. Beanne: 7:00 p.m., 2 hours
Mr. Hobbs: 5:00 p.m., 3 hours
Mrs. Samuels: 5:30 p.m., 2 1/2 hours
Mrs. Jones: 6:00 p.m., 1 1/2 hours
Salty's alibi is substantiated.

7.2 SECOND ALIBI

Oscar: book store, walked
Nelmira: sewing shop, bus
Jewel: music store, cab
Airedale: pizza parlor, car

7.3 WITNESSES

Mr. Jay: music store, 7:00 p.m.
Mrs. Pill: sewing shop, 7:15 p.m.
Mr. Toms: pizza parlor, 8:15 p.m.
Mr. Johns: book store, 6:45 p.m.
Airedale's alibi is substantiated.

8.1 FACTS ABOUT THE MESSAGE

Answers will vary.

8.2 THE MESSAGE

Decoding key: shift two letters to the left

Message: the recipe is mine time to get what we want use plan A

Decoding key: shift 12 letters to the right.

Message: you are becoming quite a detective

9.1 NOTES FROM DETECTIVE ABEL

Jewel: Type-Better model 457, distorted "e"

Oscar: No Error model 240, broken "g"

Nelmira: Type-O model 124, distorted "y"

Jewel Treasure is the culprit.

PRACTICE PUZZLES

1. SUSPECTS QUESTIONED

Jewel: third

Salty: sixth

Nelmira: fifth

Elbarno: second

Airedale: first

Oscar: fourth

2. WHO QUESTIONED WHOM?

Airedale: Gray

Salty: Jones

Jewel: Woods

Elbarno: White

Nelmira: Brown

Oscar: Smith

3. SUSPECTS' APPEARANCES

Oscar: gray hair, brown eyes

Nelmira: brown hair, blue eyes

Jewel: red hair, hazel eyes

Airedale: blond hair, green eyes

4. BIRTH MONTHS

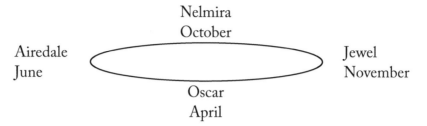

Nelmira
October

Airedale
June

Jewel
November

Oscar
April

5. POLICE TALK

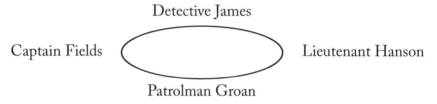

Detective James

Captain Fields

Lieutenant Hanson

Patrolman Groan

6. WHERE THEY'RE FROM

Airedale: Dallas
Salty: New York
Jewel: Miami
Nelmira: Boston
Oscar: Philadelphia

7. SALTY AND HIS REUNION

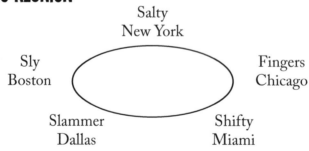

Salty
New York

Sly
Boston

Fingers
Chicago

Slammer
Dallas

Shifty
Miami

8. PIZZA BUT NO CHOCOLATE

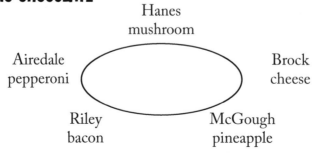

Hanes
mushroom

Airedale
pepperoni

Brock
cheese

Riley
bacon

McGough
pineapple

9. POLICE REPORTS—MIDDLE NAMES

Salty: Hunter
Nelmira: Taylor
Elbarno: Walker
Airedale: Bruce
Oscar: Spencer

10. YEARS IN THE CITY

Airedale: 22 years
Salty: 2 years
Jewel: 11 years
Elbarno: 25 years
Nelmira: 15 years
Oscar: 30 years

11. TRAFFIC VIOLATIONS

Airedale: ran a stop sign
Elbarno: made an illegal left turn
Nelmira: was caught speeding
Oscar: ran a red light

12. IDENTIFYING MARKS

Jewel: 5'10", cowlick
Nelmira: 5'1", mole
Elbarno: 5'9", scar
Airedale: 5'7", widow's peak
Oscar: 6'5", birthmark
Salty: 4'11", crooked finger

13. WHAT THEY WERE WEARING

Jewel: purple vest
Nelmira: brown bathrobe
Elbarno: red sweater
Airedale: black sweatshirt
Oscar: green shirt
Salty: blue jacket

14. HOBBIES AND AWARDS

Salty: postcards, poetry
Nelmira: gardening, clarinet
Jewel: guitar, debate
Elbarno: stamps, track
Oscar: models, swimming
Airedale: baseball cards, cooking

15. DISTANCE TO THE POLICE STATION

1st street: Whit Boulevard, Nelmira

2nd street: Elm Street, Salty

3rd street: Stuart Avenue, Elbarno

4th street: Bremo Road, Jewel

5th street: Clair Drive, Airedale

6th street: Kent Road, Oscar

16. HOME SWEET HOME

Airedale: ranch
Salty: boardinghouse
Jewel: duplex
Elbarno: mansion
Nelmira: cottage
Oscar: apartment

17. HOUSE EXTERIORS

Airedale: white aluminum
Salty: beige vinyl
Jewel: yellow stucco
Elbarno: gray brick
Nelmira: brown cedar
Oscar: red clapboard

18. SHOESTRING MALL

food court	toys	chocolates	north entrance	pets	50 Cent		department store
	shoes	books	south entrance	dresses	frames		

19. FOOD COURT

chicken	corn dogs	deli
french fries		
cookies		
pizza	chili	ice cream

20. FACTORY ROW

Chew-Easy Dog Biscuits	Lint-Free Sweaters	Keep-Warm Coats	Elbarno Chocolates
Dutch Delight Chocolates	Big-Head Hats	Stay-Afloat Swim Wear	Fit-Well Shoes

21. SECOND FLOOR AT THE CHOCOLATE FACTORY

kitchen	lounge	conference
supply	elevator	file room
lab	Mrs. Castleberry	Van Feisty

THE MYSTERY UNWINDS

The suspects are eliminated with information presented in the following lessons:

3.1: Imelda Castleberry, Barry Newell, Benny Bartholomew

6.2: Elbarno Farnsworth

7.1: Salty the Cracker

7.2 and 7.3: Airedale Johnson

8.1, 8.2, and 9.1: Oscar Hobson and Nelmira Simpson are eliminated, and Jewel Treasure is implicated as the guilty person.

ABOUT THE AUTHOR

An educator for 27 years, Mary Ann Carr has taught grades K–7. In addition to working in the classroom, she was a resource teacher for a Chapter 1 program in an inner-city school and a gifted specialist in a large suburban school system. This wide range of experience provided the seed for her passion for differentiation and her understanding of issues facing teachers out in the trenches.

Carr found that teachers generally lack two things—time and materials. Taking into account these and other concerns voiced by teachers, Carr began developing instructional materials to make their jobs easier. Frequently asked to present in workshops and at state conferences, she promotes differentiation through humorous and motivational presentations that provide practical tools teachers can use to meet the diverse needs of their students. She is the author of *Differentiation Made Simple*, a book that helps teachers implement differentiation strategies in the classroom.

Carr is also the author of *One-Hour Mysteries*, *More One-Hour Mysteries*, and *The Private Eye School*, all published by Prufrock Press. These CSI-like mysteries require students to engage in critical thinking while having fun solving crimes in the classroom.